Time Sheet

DATE		TIME IN	TIME OUT	TOTAL HOURS

Time Sheet

Name _____

Month/Year _____

DATE		TIME IN	TIME OUT	TOTAL HOURS

Time Sheet

Name _____

Month/Year |_____

DATE		TIME IN	TIME OUT	TOTAL HOURS

Time Sheet

Name _____

Month/Year _____

DATE		TIME IN	TIME OUT	TOTAL HOURS

Time Sheet

Name _____

Month/Year _____

DATE		TIME IN	TIME OUT	TOTAL HOURS

Time Sheet

Name

Month/Year

DATE		TIME IN	TIME OUT	TOTAL HOURS

Time Sheet

Name

Month/Year

DATE		TIME IN	TIME OUT	TOTAL HOURS

Time Sheet

Name

Month/Year

DATE		TIME IN	TIME OUT	TOTAL HOURS

Time Sheet

Name

Month/Year

DATE		TIME IN	TIME OUT	TOTAL HOURS

Time Sheet

Name _____

Month/Year _____

DATE		TIME IN	TIME OUT	TOTAL HOURS

Time Sheet

DATE		TIME IN	TIME OUT	TOTAL HOURS

Time Sheet

Name

Month/Year

DATE		TIME IN	TIME OUT	TOTAL HOURS

Time Sheet

Name _____

Month/Year _____

DATE		TIME IN	TIME OUT	TOTAL HOURS

Time Sheet

Name

Month/Year

DATE		TIME IN	TIME OUT	TOTAL HOURS

Time Sheet

Name

Month/Year

DATE		TIME IN	TIME OUT	TOTAL HOURS

Time Sheet

Name

Month/Year

DATE		TIME IN	TIME OUT	TOTAL HOURS

Time Sheet

Name

Month/Year

DATE		TIME IN	TIME OUT	TOTAL HOURS

Time Sheet

Name

Month/Year

DATE		TIME IN	TIME OUT	TOTAL HOURS

Time Sheet

Name

Month/Year

DATE		TIME IN	TIME OUT	TOTAL HOURS

Time Sheet

Name

Month/Year

DATE		TIME IN	TIME OUT	TOTAL HOURS

Time Sheet

Name _____

Month/Year _____

DATE		TIME IN	TIME OUT	TOTAL HOURS

Time Sheet

Name

Month/Year

DATE		TIME IN	TIME OUT	TOTAL HOURS

Time Sheet

Name

Month/Year

DATE		TIME IN	TIME OUT	TOTAL HOURS

Time Sheet

Name
Month/Year

DATE		TIME IN	TIME OUT	TOTAL HOURS

Time Sheet

Name
Month/Year

DATE		TIME IN	TIME OUT	TOTAL HOURS

Time Sheet

Name _____

Month/Year _____

DATE		TIME IN	TIME OUT	TOTAL HOURS

Time Sheet

Name _____

Month/Year _____

DATE		TIME IN	TIME OUT	TOTAL HOURS

Time Sheet

Name _____

Month/Year _____

DATE		TIME IN	TIME OUT	TOTAL HOURS

Time Sheet

Name

Month/Year

DATE	TIME	TIME IN	TIME OUT	TOTAL HOURS

Time Sheet

Name

Month/Year

DATE		TIME IN	TIME OUT	TOTAL HOURS

Time Sheet

Name

Month/Year

DATE		TIME IN	TIME OUT	TOTAL HOURS

Time Sheet

Name _____

Month/Year _____

DATE		TIME IN	TIME OUT	TOTAL HOURS

Time Sheet

Name _____

Month/Year _____

DATE		TIME IN	TIME OUT	TOTAL HOURS

Time Sheet

Name

Month/Year

DATE		TIME IN	TIME OUT	TOTAL HOURS

Time Sheet

Name _____

Month/Year _____|

DATE		TIME IN	TIME OUT	TOTAL HOURS

Time Sheet

Name _____

Month/Year |

DATE		TIME IN	TIME OUT	TOTAL HOURS

Time Sheet

Name _____

Month/Year _____

DATE		TIME IN	TIME OUT	TOTAL HOURS

Time Sheet

Name _____

Month/Year _____

DATE		TIME IN	TIME OUT	TOTAL HOURS

Time Sheet

Name

Month/Year

DATE		TIME IN	TIME OUT	TOTAL HOURS

Time Sheet

Name _____

Month/Year _____

DATE		TIME IN	TIME OUT	TOTAL HOURS

Time Sheet

Name _____

Month/Year _____

DATE		TIME IN	TIME OUT	TOTAL HOURS

Time Sheet

Name

Month/Year

DATE		TIME IN	TIME OUT	TOTAL HOURS

Time Sheet

Name

Month/Year

DATE		TIME IN	TIME OUT	TOTAL HOURS

Time Sheet

Name

Month/Year

DATE		TIME IN	TIME OUT	TOTAL HOURS

Time Sheet

Name
Month/Year

DATE		TIME IN	TIME OUT	TOTAL HOURS

Time Sheet

Name

Month/Year

DATE		TIME IN	TIME OUT	TOTAL HOURS

Time Sheet

Name _____
Month/Year _____

DATE		TIME IN	TIME OUT	TOTAL HOURS

Time Sheet

Name _____

Month/Year _____

DATE		TIME IN	TIME OUT	TOTAL HOURS

Time Sheet

Name _____

Month/Year _____

DATE		TIME IN	TIME OUT	TOTAL HOURS

Time Sheet

Name _____

Month/Year _____

DATE		TIME IN	TIME OUT	TOTAL HOURS

Time Sheet

Name

Month/Year

DATE		TIME IN	TIME OUT	TOTAL HOURS

Time Sheet

Name _____

Month/Year _____

DATE		TIME IN	TIME OUT	TOTAL HOURS

Time Sheet

Name _____

Month/Year _____

DATE		TIME IN	TIME OUT	TOTAL HOURS

Time Sheet

Name

Month/Year

DATE		TIME IN	TIME OUT	TOTAL HOURS

Time Sheet

Name

Month/Year

DATE		TIME IN	TIME OUT	TOTAL HOURS

Time Sheet

Name _____

Month/Year |

DATE		TIME IN	TIME OUT	TOTAL HOURS

Time Sheet

Name _____

Month/Year _____

DATE		TIME IN	TIME OUT	TOTAL HOURS

Time Sheet

Name _____

Month/Year _____

DATE		TIME IN	TIME OUT	TOTAL HOURS

Time Sheet

Name
Month/Year

DATE		TIME IN	TIME OUT	TOTAL HOURS

Time Sheet

Name

Month/Year

DATE		TIME IN	TIME OUT	TOTAL HOURS

Time Sheet

Name _____
Month/Year _____

DATE		TIME IN	TIME OUT	TOTAL HOURS

Time Sheet

Name

Month/Year

DATE		TIME IN	TIME OUT	TOTAL HOURS

Time Sheet

Name _____

Month/Year _____

DATE		TIME IN	TIME OUT	TOTAL HOURS

Time Sheet

Name

Month/Year

DATE		TIME IN	TIME OUT	TOTAL HOURS

Time Sheet

Name _____

Month/Year _____

DATE		TIME IN	TIME OUT	TOTAL HOURS

Time Sheet

Name

Month/Year

DATE		TIME IN	TIME OUT	TOTAL HOURS

Time Sheet

Name _____

Month/Year _____

DATE		TIME IN	TIME OUT	TOTAL HOURS

Time Sheet

Name _____
Month/Year _____

DATE		TIME IN	TIME OUT	TOTAL HOURS

Time Sheet

Name _____

Month/Year _____

DATE		TIME IN	TIME OUT	TOTAL HOURS

Time Sheet

Name _____

Month/Year _____

DATE		TIME IN	TIME OUT	TOTAL HOURS

Time Sheet

Name
Month/Year

DATE		TIME IN	TIME OUT	TOTAL HOURS

Time Sheet

Name _____

Month/Year _____

DATE		TIME IN	TIME OUT	TOTAL HOURS

Time Sheet

Name
Month/Year

DATE		TIME IN	TIME OUT	TOTAL HOURS

Time Sheet

Name _____

Month/Year _____

DATE		TIME IN	TIME OUT	TOTAL HOURS

Time Sheet

Name _____

Month/Year _____

DATE		TIME IN	TIME OUT	TOTAL HOURS

Time Sheet

Name

Month/Year

DATE		TIME IN	TIME OUT	TOTAL HOURS

Time Sheet

Name _____

Month/Year _____

DATE		TIME IN	TIME OUT	TOTAL HOURS

Time Sheet

Name _____

Month/Year _____

DATE		TIME IN	TIME OUT	TOTAL HOURS

Time Sheet

Name _____
Month/Year _____

DATE		TIME IN	TIME OUT	TOTAL HOURS

Time Sheet

Name

Month/Year

DATE		TIME IN	TIME OUT	TOTAL HOURS

Time Sheet

Name _____

Month/Year _____

DATE		TIME IN	TIME OUT	TOTAL HOURS

Time Sheet

Name _____
Month/Year _____

DATE		TIME IN	TIME OUT	TOTAL HOURS

Time Sheet

Name

Month/Year

DATE		TIME IN	TIME OUT	TOTAL HOURS

Time Sheet

Name _____

Month/Year _____

DATE		TIME IN	TIME OUT	TOTAL HOURS

Time Sheet

Name _____

Month/Year _____

DATE		TIME IN	TIME OUT	TOTAL HOURS

Time Sheet

Name

Month/Year

DATE		TIME IN	TIME OUT	TOTAL HOURS

Time Sheet

Name

Month/Year

DATE		TIME IN	TIME OUT	TOTAL HOURS

Time Sheet

Name
Month/Year

DATE		TIME IN	TIME OUT	TOTAL HOURS

Time Sheet

Name

Month/Year

DATE		TIME IN	TIME OUT	TOTAL HOURS

Time Sheet

Name _____
Month/Year _____

DATE		TIME IN	TIME OUT	TOTAL HOURS

Time Sheet

Name _____
Month/Year _____

DATE		TIME IN	TIME OUT	TOTAL HOURS

Time Sheet

Name _____
Month/Year _____

DATE	TIME SHEET	TIME IN	TIME OUT	TOTAL HOURS

Time Sheet

Name

Month/Year

DATE		TIME IN	TIME OUT	TOTAL HOURS

Time Sheet

Name _____

Month/Year _____

DATE		TIME IN	TIME OUT	TOTAL HOURS

Time Sheet

Name

Month/Year

DATE		TIME IN	TIME OUT	TOTAL HOURS

Time Sheet

Name

Month/Year

DATE		TIME IN	TIME OUT	TOTAL HOURS

Time Sheet

Name _____

Month/Year _____

DATE		TIME IN	TIME OUT	TOTAL HOURS

Time Sheet

Name
Month/Year

DATE		TIME IN	TIME OUT	TOTAL HOURS

Time Sheet

Name
Month/Year

DATE		TIME IN	TIME OUT	TOTAL HOURS

Time Sheet

Name

Month/Year

DATE		TIME IN	TIME OUT	TOTAL HOURS

Made in the USA
Middletown, DE
26 June 2024